Tools for Men-with-Feminist-Ambitions

M. Barner

s.L.A.p.
sabotage L.A. publishing

Tools for Men-with-Feminist-Ambitions
© Martin Barner 2021
Licensed under Creative Commons BY-NC-SA 4.0
creativecommons.org/licenses/by-nc-sa/4.0

4th edition 2024
ISBN: 978-3-9823344-0-0

s.L.A.p.

sabotage L.A. publishing
www.sabotagelapublishing.com

Assembled by Martin Barner in close collaboration with Margrit Barner, Moritz Buchholz, Laura Araujo Cornejo, Charlotte Cox, Henriette Hufgard, Camille Pellicer, Julian Prugger, Breeanne Saxton, Jaana Schnell and Johannes Sporrer.

Contents

Introduction 7

Uncertainty 11

Subjectivity 14

Radical Listening 17

Owning Emotions 21

Vulnerability 25

Attunement 28

Care Work 32

Compassionate Accountability 36

Exploring Desires 40

Interdependence 44

Antipatriarchal Solidarity 48

A Personal Note 52

Sources 56

Introduction[1]

'Asked to give up the true self in order to realize the patriarchal ideal, boys learn self-betrayal early and are rewarded for these acts of soul murder.'
– bell hooks[2]

Patriarchy frames the *basic human capacity* of emotional intimacy as feminine, everything associated with femininity as inferior (traditional sexism), and masculinity as the mutually exclusive opposite of femininity (oppositional sexism)[3]. Patriarchal masculinity is rooted in the rejection of anything that is deemed feminine, at the very least within ourselves. From us – the people who the world ruthlessly expects to personify patriarchal

---

1 This book is based on ideas developed by intersectional feminist writers (hooks, 2004; Samaran, 2019).

2 hooks, 2004, p. 153

3 Julia Serano's transfeminist work largely informed the underlying concepts of sex and gender applied in this book. She also informed the distinction between traditional and oppositional sexism, as well as the twofold discrimination of both women and femininity (Serano, 2019).

masculinity – that requires the suppression of essential parts of ourselves. Despite all the advantages that come with it, patriarchal masculinity limits what we know, say and believe, how we act and relate. It limits *who we can be*. Feminism can allow us to *recover* bits of us that we might be painfully missing.

I am granted cis, white, male, and class privileges. If I want to support, or at least not hinder the ongoing struggle of people who face injustice and discrimination on economic, institutional and legal levels, I need to also work on the ways I embody and reproduce what they are rightfully fighting against.[4]

However, we cannot 'fight' this with the strategies that we are used to. Because they themselves are shaped by patriarchal masculinity. We had to adopt it into our personality in order to get by in the world. It is deeply embedded in how we meet needs and expectations, and how we compensate if we can't.

---

4 Samaran, 2016 b

That does not mean that we are not responsible for how we affect the people and culture around us. We are. It also does not mean that we cannot change. We can. But reading or talking about certain topics, following certain rules, using a certain language, applying certain social protocols or patronising those who don't, isn't going to cut it. We also do not get out of this on our own, or only with the voices of people equally entrenched in patriarchal masculinity. Instead of turning *against ourselves* or concerning ourselves too much with who *we are*, we need to first turn *towards others*, and develop new *practices to relate* to them differently.[5]

Without a doubt, your experience is not the same as mine. Patriarchal norms intersect with many factors including class, race, gender and sexuality. While some assumptions about the reader will certainly be off, there are common patterns that we absorb or resist to, each in our own unique ways.

---

[5] The focus on the transformative potential of the 'in between' is inspired by Bini Adamczak's writing on gender and revolution (Adamczak, 2017).

This book is a collection of practices that try to develop alternatives that subvert these patterns. They are collected or developed from reading and listening to feminist activists, writers and friends. I myself continue to struggle with them fundamentally. They are at odds with patriarchal masculinity and have been systematically discouraged in us, perpetuating privilege and the harm it can cause.

Each chapter of this book focuses on one particular practice. The chapters are self-contained but best read in order. Each has three sections that roughly contain: 1. structural context for the given practice and why it is important, 2. examples or counterexamples, and 3. hands on steps to develop it further.

The contents of this book are not meant as something to know about in theory. They are also not something to work through on your own. They are intended as *interpersonal practices*, to exercise *in relation to others*.

Uncertainty

If feminism means changing who we are, we will face a lot of internal resistance and insecurity. If we have feminist ambitions for ourselves, the ability to overcome inner resistance and to hold on through uncertainty will be essential.

↓

When something causes uncertainty, we tend to deflect long before we have the chance to recognise that we were uncertain in the first place. If, for example, this text were to cause insecurity, the reaction could range from disinterest (*'I'm sure it's good but not for me'*, *'I'm not into that sort of stuff'*), dismissiveness (*'I'm all for it in general, but I disagree with this particular thing'*) to outright rejection (*'That's stupid / nonsense'*, *'I hate that / those people'*). Messaging that really goes to the core of our self or our world view can often produce such negative reactions in us. Especially in confrontation with expressivity that does not fit into classic masculinity because of its form, colour, language, topic, methodology etc., we can experience serious inner resistance. If we want to change, we need the ability to work through this avoidance and deal with the uncertainty that lies behind.

↓

1. Curiosity: Observe your own dismissiveness with curiosity. Try to notice when you immediately dismiss something you read or hear. '*That's not for me. Huh! interesting. Seems like I really don't want to engage with that. I wonder why.*' Sometimes you will only realise later on.

2. Letting go: We're taught to always appear in control of any situation. Control is incompatible with uncertainty. If you notice defensiveness in you, take a breath and try to let go of control in your head.

3. Acceptance: It's *ok* to experience the discomfort of uncertainty – you don't have to avoid, fight or 'push through' what is triggering it. Try

to acknowledge it with curiosity and without judgement – what is really causing it and how do you want to react?

4. Others: It will be much, much harder to do this alone. You literally cannot pull yourself up by your bootstraps. It's physically impossible. You cannot see your own blind spots. You need people to point them out to you and trust them enough to believe them when they do. And once the actual uncertainty sets in, you will need them to help you navigate through it. To whom can you talk about these topics openly? ($\rightarrow$ Vulnerability)

5. Chase the uncomfortable: The things that really make us change are by definition slightly uncomfortable. Once you get used to noticing when things make you defensive, you can make it a habit to pay attention to them.

Subjectivity[6]

Patriarchal masculinity means generally trusting your own perception over others'. Usually, we do not think of our own perception as distinct from reality, or that it would require listening, thinking and communicating to match it up with the perspective of others. If we were wrong, it's because we lacked information, not because our perception was unreliable or biased. However, since perceptions differ, our certainty is possible only if everyone else adjusts to us. If someone else insists on their view in ways we don't understand, they must have misunderstood or not heard us, be crazy, unreasonable or 'too emotional'. This is not only enabling abusive behaviour, but we collectively and continuously undermine others' trust in their perception (gaslighting), which *in itself* is abusive and harmful.

---

6 This chapter is inspired by Nora Samaran's Essay 'On Gaslighting' (Samaran, 2016 a).

↓

A: *'I'm scared.'*
B: *'Don't worry!'*

Person B assumes that person A's perception (something is dangerous) and their emotional reaction are wrong, and that B's (nothing to worry) is correct. B declares their perception as the new truth for both that now dominates, especially if A has had the trust in their perception systematically undermined in this way. Person A might continue to feel uneasy, but some part of them will question their own reality: *'Was I wrong? Did I overreact? I cannot trust my own senses.'* and they will learn: *'I cannot rely on B to believe me when needed.'* If you 'believe' others, but still trust your perception of their situation more than their own, they will not feel or be much safer with you around. We need to value our own perception as the *subjective* experience it is, so we can trust and reaffirm the perspectives of others.

↓

1. Fake it 'till you make it: Start accepting others' perception 'hypothetically' and act accordingly. You could start with this text. If something written doesn't match your perspective, assume you're wrong, not the text – just for a while. What's the worst that could happen?

2. Apply → Radical Listening whenever you get a chance. Listen especially to people with experiences different from yours, and especially on issues involving yourself.

3. Don't go alone: Sincerely and continuously viewing our perception as fallible will come with an uncertainty and confusion we are not used to. If possible, find one or more trusted friends to practice with and to rely on each other when things get confusing.

Radical Listening[7]

A: '*My bike got stolen. I'm an idiot, I didn't lock it.*'
B: '*No wonder it got stolen then!*'

Patriarchal masculinity hears without listening, which actively blocks any opportunity for emotions to be processed. They *will* come out elsewhere, possibly in harmful behaviour. We often unconsciously displace emotions onto others who must carefully guess and manage those feelings for us in order to stay safe; less privileged groups are then encumbered with a disproportionate amount of listening work. We must instead practice providing that space, especially for each other.

↓

Through radical listening, we want to not only hear but understand another's feelings and reflect them back with acceptance. The active reflection

---

[7] The concept of 'radical listening' was developed by Sarah Hempstock and Soofiya Andry in the context of racism in the US (Hempstock & Andry, 2017).

allows the speaker to see their own situation from another point of view, thereby making space for the recognition, acceptance and ownership of feelings.

A: *'My bike got stolen. I'm an idiot, didn't lock it.'*

B: *'Sorry. You loved that bike. Are you angry that you didn't lock it?'*

A: *'I'm ashamed, I guess. It's like I can't get anything right.'*

B: *'Understandable. It's a lot of pressure to get it all right all the time.'*

↓

1. When: Radical listening is good whenever emotions are involved; when unsure, do it a bit and see if people take the offer.

2. Get consent: If being listened to is unexpected, people can risk sharing more than they're later happy with. In between, ask: '*I want to know more – are you comfortable telling me this?*'.

3. Do not 'answer'. A lot of things to say will pop up in your head: opinions, advice, interpretations,

solutions, judgements, excuses, explanations and related stories. Ignore them all. As they pop up, accept that for now, they will not be heard. Return your focus to hearing the other person. In radical listening you are valuable to them because you really *listen*, not because you *say* something valuable or offer a 'solution'.

4. Try to understand: Try to truly understand what is going on and assume that you don't. Do not interrupt. If they halt, summarise what you think they said. Then ask: '*Did I understand that correctly?*'. Then wait for them to continue.

5. Empathise: As they speak, try to get a sense of how they *feel* about what they say (→ Attunement). If you can't, keep asking; keep trying to understand where they are coming from.

6. Offer possible feelings: Do not tell them how they feel but offer suggestions: '*Sounds unfair. Were you angry?*'; '*I think I would have been very scared but also excited – how was that for you?*'. Things related to negative feelings are

often shared as if they were an unimportant side note. Listen carefully for those.

7. Validate their expressed feelings. Say: '*It's ok to be scared. It is a scary situation.*' It is important here that you understand their perspective first and feel them enough to then say this honestly and from the heart.

8. Add perspective: Only *after* you have fully listened, empathised with their situation and taken how they feel about it seriously, maybe offer an alternative outlook. If you are not sure what to say, '*thank you for sharing this with me*' is a perfectly acceptable response.

Owning Emotions[8]

Emotions give you essential information about your physical and social environment and how it relates to you. Feeling any emotion very generally is *safe* – no harm will come to you from feeling an emotion alone. Furthermore, emotions – if not suppressed – are temporary. They always pass. Most importantly, feeling emotions does not force you to act 'emotionally'. Ironically, if we *suppress* emotions, they will affect our behaviour *unconsciously*. Patriarchy falsely portrays that as more 'rational'. It obscures and justifies the often harmful consequences and places the burden of working around these emotionally driven behaviours onto others. If we instead feel and own our emotions, we can contextualise the information and consciously decide how we want to react to them.

---

[8] This chapter is largely informed by letters received from Berlin based therapist Jaana Schnell, who introduces subversive sexual, queer and non-monogamous knowledge into psychotherapy.

↓

If you think, '*I don't really get sad*' (or angry, scared, anxious, etc.) or if you hardly ever cry, this likely applies to you. You have likely been pushed to suppress some part of yourself from such a young age that you think it either doesn't exist or that it is better or safer to not give it any space at all.

↓

To get closer to your emotions, do the following regularly:

1. Notice when you should pay particular attention to your emotions: When you procrastinate or distract yourself a lot; when you 'overreact'; when you behave in unexpected ways; when you get unusually emotional over something you see or hear.

2. Spend time alone without distraction regularly: Go for a walk, or sit alone (home, bar, cafe, park) to write, draw or just think – experiment

what works for you. Go over things that have happened. As you do, try to notice any changes in how your body feels. If any thoughts cause a reaction, go over them in more detail. The first time you do this, you might end up considering how stupid this is. Good start!

3. Talk: Emotions come out and transform when they are heard. Is something bothering you? Try speaking about it with someone ($\rightarrow$ Vulnerability). If you have an inner resistance to doing that – that's patriarchy at work. Fight it! You do not need to have anything figured out beforehand – '*I feel weird somehow, can we talk?*' is enough.

4. Own: Using these tools to recognise and manage your feelings and how you *decide* to respond to them is *your* responsibility. Remember that 1. Not acknowledging your feelings can cause harm to yourself and - especially if you are privileged - to others. 2. By listening to your feelings, you *no longer have to act* according to them. You could even do the opposite of what they suggest. Or just hold on to them until they pass.

3. If feelings are related to other people's behaviour, they are still your responsibility. '*You make me angry*' defies responsibility – '*I get angry when ...*' gives you agency.

Vulnerability[9]

Vulnerability is a powerful act of self-expression that creates connection and trust. It can mean showing 'weakness', sharing things we are ashamed of or expressing important feelings. It means asking someone to listen, and maybe requesting support, emotional or otherwise. It is a core skill to build trust and intimacy in friendship and romance.

In patriarchal masculinity, '*be a man*' is synonym for '*don't show vulnerability*'. Although emotional strength requires vulnerability, it is falsely considered weak, and weakness is shamed. That promotes appearing 'autonomous' and self-reliant, and to ignore feelings such as loneliness, fear, confusion, insecurity, hurt or shame. If you don't usually turn towards others (and others towards you) in emotionally intense moments, then this likely applies to you.

---

9 Judith Butler established a nuanced discourse on the gendered and political dimensions of vulnerability (Butler et al, 2016). It is also central to Mark Greene's work on masculinity (Greene, 2016).

↓

If we don't reach out and express when we are hurt, upset or struggling, these buried feelings often spill into the lives of others: We might project our needs onto them (*'My partner can't handle me working late every day'*, *'You're too needy'*, *'You must be cold'*), making it hard to care for them with → Attunement. We might retreat (*'I usually deal with things on my own.'*, *'I don't want to talk about it'*, *'I need to be alone.'*), dismiss (*'I'm fine.'*) or distract ourselves and procrastinate. We might turn to anger, violence or self-harm (for example hitting a wall). Finally, our vulnerabilities might have no outlet at all, leading to isolation or health issues. As we avoid vulnerability, the people around us must do all the → Care Work to guess our needs, out of love or to stay safe.

↓

1. Write down things that an imagined, more emotional version of yourself would currently be scared of, worried about, struggle with or be ashamed of.

2. Who would you be most comfortable sharing one of these things with? We need people who can accept our vulnerability without interrupting, overreacting or being dismissive. Vulnerability is what builds the deep trust it requires, so you might have to take a small leap of faith here.

3. Imagine telling them about one of the things. If that idea is not uncomfortable, pick something more difficult. If it is too much, pick an easier one. Inspect the discomfort curiously. Where does it come from?

4. Call the person right now. Ask if you could share something personal. If they give you a clear yes, tell them about the thing. This takes strength. We need to wade through inner resistance and possibly shame. It means speaking slowly or awkwardly, without knowing immediately what to say, or how to say it.

5. Review: How did they react? How did that make you feel?

Attunement[10]

When actor Aziz Ansari went home with a young photographer, that person later described the evening as '*the worst night of [her] life*' to the media.[11] He responded that he had '*misread things in the moment*' and was '*surprised and concerned*' hearing about it. How is it possible that one person has the worst night of her life, and the other apparently does not *notice at all*? If we believe him, there must have been a complete emotional disconnect. Our goal has to be not only to prevent that, but to do the *opposite*: consistently interact with others in an *attuned* way, so that we are an active source of safety and not a threat. '*Attuned*' means being 'in tune' with others emotionally without overreaching, so we can interact with them appropriately: giving practical advice

---

10 I found 'attunement' in Nora Samaran's writing, who brings it from attachment style theory (Johnson, 2011) into feminist discourse (Samaran, 2019).

11 The story was confirmed by Ansari (Way, 2018).

or listening; taking their hand or stepping away; reaching out or leaving them alone.

↓

She says to him: '*X was waiting for me outside my house*'. She acts calm but is scared.

If he is not attuned to her, he might not pick up on her emotional state (*'Ah, X! How is he?'*), fail to listen (*'Yeah, one time I …'*), minimise (*'He's just a bit weird!'*), dismiss her accurate perception (*'Don't worry, he's nice!'*), feel for her, blinding him to what she needs (*'I'll punch him!'*), distance himself through pity (*'I'm sorry for you'*) or jump to a 'solution' (*'Call the police!'*).

↓

There is no protocol for an attuned response. We need to:

1. Recognise when attunement is especially important: for consent (→ Exploring Desires); when someone is showing → Vulnerability; when someone is in distress.

2. → Subjectivity & → Uncertainty: We cannot seem in control of a situation and 'know exactly what to do' and at the same time be reactive to others. Exhale and mentally let go of control. Actively open up to where the other person leads you. You may feel vulnerable (→ Vulnerability) – you're ready to connect!

3. → Owning Emotions: When suppressing your emotions, you also suppress your empathetic sense for someone else. Listen to *your* feelings.

4. Actively see and listen to the person: What exactly are they saying? Do they look worried, excited, scared, absent? Is how they look aligned with what they say / do? Enter a general attitude of focus, attention and curiosity towards their emotional state: 'tune in' with them.

5. Boundaries: The feeling that then arises is a *mix* of how we feel and how they feel. For attunement we need to know, which is which. If someone is panicking, you want to sense their panic, but not break out into panic yourself. Attunement

meets distress with calm, not nervousness; hurt with compassion, not anger; shame with love, not embarrassment. This does *not* mean to suppress those feelings; just to be conscious about *who* you are feeling for, which will change *what* you feel.

6. Ask: An attuned connection is always imperfect. Complement attunement with clarifying questions and → Radical Listening.

Care Work[12]

Care work is the work of tracking, managing and doing the tasks necessary to meet the emotional and physical needs of ourselves and others. This includes taking responsibility to nurture and repair social connections. Patriarchy frames this as something that femininity supposedly naturally *is*, rather than *work* that somebody *does*. It disregards both its importance and the skills involved, robbing a tremendous amount of time and energy from the people doing most of the care work, without an appropriate material compensation. This can make it difficult for those with the privilege to offload it onto others to recognise, prioritise and learn it: Masculinity is supposed to draw self-worth solely from a never-ending, self-centred pursuit of status and goals, not from contributing to a functioning interdependent life.

---

12 Care work is a long-standing (Ferguson, 2019) and current (Hutchinson, 2017; Doyle, 2019) concept in broader feminist discussion on economics, class and labour.

↓

Care work can be *personal* (i.e. taking time for yourself; going to the dentist), *interpersonal* (i.e. communicating your needs clearly; tracking important events in the lives of people around you; initiating conversations about relationships; → Radical Listening), *communal* (preventing and mediating conflict; caring for children in your vicinity; managing household maintenance; teaching; collaborating and considering everyone's perspective when organising group events), *societal* (political groundwork), or even *global* (educating yourself on global issues; adopting a sustainable way of live; fighting climate collapse). How much *time and energy* do you put into these tasks? How much work do you put into *learning* to do them? What thoughts and feelings come up when you consider truly prioritising care work at the expense of your social status or personal goals?

↓

1. Self-care:[13] If you tend to disregard your own needs, caring for others can sound overwhelming (→ Interdependence). Start with doing your share in making sure your *own* interdependent needs are met: Practice identifying them (→ Owning Emotions), and proactively requesting support (→ Vulnerability). Doing this consistently can already lift a burden off both you and those around you.

2. Collaboration: Care work cannot be done alone or even on your own terms. If you often 'decide' for others what they 'need' from you, rather than doing what *they actually need*, being asked to do 'even more' can make you feel helpless, unseen and taken for granted. What are you doing for yourself or others that isn't aligned with actual needs? What are you *not* doing that *is* needed? The only reliable way to find out is to *ask* and

---

13 Audre Lorde popularised the concept of self-care (Lorde, 1988) as political 'self-preservation' in the face of intersectional discrimination.

↓

Care work can be *personal* (i.e. taking time for yourself; going to the dentist), *interpersonal* (i.e. communicating your needs clearly; tracking important events in the lives of people around you; initiating conversations about relationships; → Radical Listening), *communal* (preventing and mediating conflict; caring for children in your vicinity; managing household maintenance; teaching; collaborating and considering everyone's perspective when organising group events), *societal* (political groundwork), or even *global* (educating yourself on global issues; adopting a sustainable way of live; fighting climate collapse). How much *time and energy* do you put into these tasks? How much work do you put into *learning* to do them? What thoughts and feelings come up when you consider truly prioritising care work at the expense of your social status or personal goals?

↓

1. Self-care:[13] If you tend to disregard your own needs, caring for others can sound overwhelming (→ Interdependence). Start with doing your share in making sure your *own* interdependent needs are met: Practice identifying them (→ Owning Emotions), and proactively requesting support (→ Vulnerability). Doing this consistently can already lift a burden off both you and those around you.

2. Collaboration: Care work cannot be done alone or even on your own terms. If you often 'decide' for others what they 'need' from you, rather than doing what *they actually need*, being asked to do 'even more' can make you feel helpless, unseen and taken for granted. What are you doing for yourself or others that isn't aligned with actual needs? What are you *not* doing that *is* needed? The only reliable way to find out is to *ask* and

---

[13] Audre Lorde popularised the concept of self-care (Lorde, 1988) as political 'self-preservation' in the face of intersectional discrimination.

take the responses seriously – use → Subjectivity, → Radical Listening and → Attunement.

3. Take Responsibility: Only with the privilege to offload care work onto others or evade responsibility if it doesn't get done can you say: *'I want to, but I don't have the skills / time / energy / resources'*. Recognise that not doing your fair share of care work is a choice you make. What small or big (individual and collective) steps could you take *now* to allow you to include a fair share of care work into your life in the long run? Discuss these decisions with anyone affected by them.

Compassionate Accountability[14]

Patriarchy makes the pervasive harm it produces invisible or isolates it as inherent to some stigmatised individuals: 'perpetrators', 'victims', 'sexists'. The opposite is *accountability*: acknowledging, owning, ending, and when possible repairing and preventing widespread harm. Without → Vulnerability, masculinity can respond to getting harmed only with fleeing, enduring or *attacking*. As a result, we do not recognise the value of accountability. Altogether this robs us of the conditions we need for accountability.

↓

The visceral reactions that avoid accountability are isolating and invalidating, and often as harmful as the original violation: First, *dismissing*:

---

14 This derives from and responds to the concept of 'community accountability', collectively developed by communities facing discrimination and state violence including black, and indigenous and women of color (Bierria, 2012).

ignoring (*'Not my place to intervene.'*, *'It's bad but what can I do.'*), normalising (*'What did you expect.'*), questioning (*'Did it really happen like this?'*, *'They wouldn't do that.'*), invalidating (*'I was joking.'*), minimising (*'I'm fine.'*) and all-or-nothing thinking (*'I'm not a sexist!'*, *'Women can't rape.'*). When harm does get acknowledged, a common reaction is to *divert focus* from harm to the 'trouble' of dealing with it (*'I feel bad when you say I hurt you.'*, *'Don't make a scene.'*, *'You're bad for the team.'*, *'Stay out of it.'*). Even if focus remains on the harm, we *divert responsibility* to the environment (*'They never learned better.'*, *'I did this because when I was a child ...'*), or even those that get harmed (*'They shouldn't have gone home with them'*, *'You make me so upset.'*). A last resort is to *essentialise* and shame, making inflicting harm seem like a character trait rather than a choice (*'I'm trying my best'* *'I'm a bad person'*, *'You're sexist'*, *'They are a rapist'*, *'Boys will be boys'*).

↓

1. Expect → Uncertainty: We have no generalisable protocols for accountability. You will not know the right steps to take – you will need to go through internal resistance *towards* uncertainty. Accountability means taking risks, improvising, making mistakes and starting interactions with uncertain outcomes.

2. Acknowledge and commit: Take a moment to consider that *good people cause harm all the time* and honestly think about those around you: where does *something* feel *off*? Did someone mention harm (Use → Subjectivity)? Include behaviour from and towards you. Work through deterring thoughts.

3. Empower those in harm's way: Their needs and safety must be the number one priority. Listen (→ Radical Listening) to them with → Attunement. Resist any urge to minimise, excuse or explain the harm done (especially when you caused it). Instead, clearly acknowledge it to the

people involved and commit to action: *'This is not okay. I want to do something'*. Don't jump to your own solutions, find out how you can *assist them* in regaining their agency.

4. Be compassionate: Uncompromisingly challenge harmful *behaviour*, but without judging the *person*: *'What's going on for you? [listens]. I accept you as a person, but not your actions'*. Get support – from whom can you expect a compassionate response when you say: *'I am hurting someone. I need your help.'*? Talk to them about holding each other accountable.

When it comes to physical or emotional abuse, Compassionate Accountability is likely not a safe, sufficient or appropriate response. If at all possible, seek out professional support or ask someone you trust to help you do so, whatever your role in the situation is. If you are unsure if someone's behaviour qualifies as abuse, that is enough to treat it as such.

Exploring Desires[15]

In patriarchy, most interactions follow a non-consensual script – take sex as an example: Masculinity is expected to consistently *want*, *'get'* and *'perform well'* at so-called penetrative sex by appearing confidently in control. You supposedly *'take'* it by convincing others to incrementally stop resisting ('give their consent'). The pressure on this can be huge since it is the only source of intimacy that is compatible with masculinity (→ Interdependence). In this script, masculinity 'consents' by merely existing – and rarely *experiences* consent. Its role is to push forward in a one-dimensional progression, disregarding its own consent. This collaterally blinds it to others' consent, which the script reduces to easily dismissible, binary yes / no answers.

---

[15] The concept of sexual consent was first developed in BDSM and kink communities (Meltsner, 2017). The approach used here is mostly based on the work of Dr. Meg-John Barker (Barker, 2020) as well as relationship anarchy (Bee, 2004), which partially originates from asexual and aromantic communities (Nordgren, 2006).

↓

'Consent' then can get obscured or become superficial: We respond to perceived expectations (*'Can I touch you there?'*) or perceived bids for ego validation (*'Does this feel good?' 'Do you like this?'*). We falsely assume escalation of consent from a previous 'step' (from eye contact to conversation, to touch, to kissing etc.). We delegate consent, letting a label or a third party dictate it (*'That's what couples do', 'Not with my ex!', 'Keep your partner happy', 'Can I do ... with your partner?'*). Consent gets obscured if it can have serious consequences (in power relations; when risking withdrawal of attention, love, or resources). Finally, people may dissociate (they are not present and unable to sense or express desires, to override hesitation or as a trauma response).

↓

For an exploration of mutual desires, combine the following:

1. Contextual awareness: Is everyone in a good position to express their desires freely and without consequences? → Subjectivity is important here – what seems safe to you may not be for others.

2. Tuning in: Practice self-consent[16] – picture things you (dis)like (nothing too intense). How do you feel each desire / aversion in your body? With others around, actively relax and try to let go of control, roles and expectations (if you can't, say it – *'I'm not present, can we slow down?'*). Then you can tune in with others (→ Attunement): How do they feel? Are you all *present* and *positively enthusiastic* each moment? Step back if anything feels off. When you want something uncomfortable, do it consciously and discuss it first.

3. Talking: Exchange felt desires with *words*. If your priority is not to get what you want (*'Can I ...?'*), but to genuinely identify *mutual* desires, you express yours honestly, ask *open* questions and make declining easy (*'I want to continue this*

---

[16] The idea of self-consent was developed by Dr. Sophia Graham (Graham, 2017).

conversation, but I'm cold. What do you feel like?', *'I'm uncomfortable with this'*, *'I'd love doing exactly this exactly like that with you. I'd be curious what you're into if you want to tell me at some point.'*, *'Do you want ... or ... or ... or something else?'*).

4. Consent culture: You cannot suddenly jump into consensual practice in particular situations – it only works if you adopt it as a *general attitude in everyday life*, building a consensual culture around you.

Interdependence[17]

Although humans need other people for *everything* (from intimacy and emotional safety to everything we produce and consume), patriarchal masculinity is supposed to look 'independent' and 'autonomous' (with the exception of sex or a single romantic relationship). This paradox is masked through privilege: People can only be 'lone wolves' or 'providers' who themselves 'don't really need anyone' in a world that ignores and invalidates the resulting → Care Work and pain this creates for others.

By disacknowledging dependence, we do not 'protect' our autonomy or become less of a 'burden' – we create emotional scarcity: *'I cannot help you meet your insatiable needs because mine are not met either'*. Real autonomy arises from the emotional abundance we build if we normalise

---

[17] This chapter is inspired by Nora Samaran's essay 'The Opposite of Rape Culture is Nurturance Culture' (Samaran, 2019). It draws heavily on attachment style theory (Johnson, 2011) and non-monogamous practice (Fern, 2020).

interdependence: *'It's normal that we need (often simple) things from each other. Let's hear them and see where we meet.'*

↓

Masculinity overstretches sex and romance to fulfil all emotional needs. To uphold the illusion of independence, we project needs and the responsibility for them onto others (*'You are needy'*, *'You make me feel ..., you have to ...'*, *'I did ... because you ...'*), send mixed signals between words, body language and behaviour, don't say directly what we (don't) want and attack, flee, or freeze when asked directly. Our boundaries – where our needs and limits meet those of others – become brittle: rigid (not considering the needs / limits of others) and easily collapsing (not considering our own needs / limits).

↓

1. Acknowledge needs and limits as normal, and negative emotions as important information about them. Where does something feel uneasy

(→ Owning Emotions)? What is (not) happening that you (don't) want? Get to the core of it (*'I need love and support'* rather than *'I need a partner'*). This may seem pointless or bring up harsh realities if this is new – take it slow and be kind to yourself.

2. Discern responsibility: Knowing and respecting your needs (and the limits of others) is *your* responsibility. Nobody is obliged to agree to something that involves you or to *not agree to something that does not involve you* and vice versa. This gets mixed up easily: When you think *'I need you to (not) want / feel / need ...'*, *'You want / feel / need ...'*, work out *your* underlying feelings and needs.

3. Communicate: Owning your needs and limits opens the space to collaborate honestly. Use → Radical Listening to hear others' needs and → Vulnerability to express yours.

4. Practice → Compassionate Accountability as limits and boundaries continue to get crossed despite our best efforts.

5. Emotional abundance: As the emotional needs in and around us will be met more consistently, they become easier and easier to express and fulfil, until a sense of safety and freedom arises from emotional abundance.

Antipatriarchal Solidarity[18]

Patriarchal 'masculinity' equals masculine *'superiority'* – being *above others* in some way. That makes it *precarious*[19] by definition – it is easily lost and must constantly be proven through hostile action. It is gained in a competition to create, expose and punish a supposed 'less than' in others. This 'less than' makes patriarchal masculinity *oppressive* and *exclusionary*: 'less than' is equated with 'feminine' or 'gay', and anyone who is not a 'man' in patriarchal terms is a potential target by definition. Finally, it is *compulsory*. If we consistently lose, ignore or openly oppose patriarchal masculinity, we risk being seen as 'feminine' and supposedly inferior. Patriarchy tries to turn us against each other to punish those who don't perpetuate it.

---

18 The notion of solidarity used here tries to consider at least in parts the complex feminist discours around solidarity (Bargetz et al, 2019), and draws on Jodi Dean's writing on 'reflective solidarity' in particular (Dean, 1995). Masculine pecking orders as discussed here are a central theme in Mark Greene's work (Greene, 2016, 2018).

19 Vandello et al, 2008

As a result, we cannot stop that wheel individually. We need to make risky but hopeful offers of solidarity. When those offers are accepted, a small space opens where it is safer to explore our connections, communities and identities outside of the limits set by patriarchal masculinity.

This antipatriarchal solidarity must explicitly extend to *all genders* - after all, it is supposed to help us move past the confines of our gendered identity. It should also be offered as much as possible to people who have not been granted much space yet to express a less patriarchal identity - they might surprise you!

↓

'Masculine superiority' creates a subtle but constant sense of unease and caution towards masculinity *for everyone*. It can turn any everyday interaction (jokes, a touch, challenges, games, asking favours, compliments, ...) into a display of 'superiority'. The urge to do so can feel like a sudden aversion, aggression, disgust, insecurity or fear towards someone specific; an impulse to brag, cross boundaries, match up, badmouth, morally judge or degrade someone; pressure to participate in something; a sense that something fun suddenly turned serious. It can also be shame, fear, insecurity or nervous admiration towards perceived assertions of superiority from others. In fear of falling behind, some try to gain a sense of superiority in more obviously harmful ways (bragging; talking over people; non-consensual touch; taking extreme risks; violence; mobbing; stalking; attacking marginalised groups).

↓

1. Pay attention to everyday moments in which you (→ Owning Emotions) or others (→ Attunement) feel challenged to show masculine 'superiority'. Be *curious* about what is going on inside you and others *without shaming* – remember that powerful mechanisms drive these behaviours.

2. Diffuse: fight the game, never the 'player' – we want to *end* the competition, not start a new one. Use → Owning Emotions (*'I feel ... but don't have to act on it'*) → Vulnerability (*'I get insecure*

when you ... can we talk about it?', 'I don't want to, this is scary.'), → Radical Listening (*'You acted weird. Are you okay?'*) and most importantly, do the → Care Work of → Compassionate accountability (whether you are the target, aggressor or witness).

3. Offer solidarity: take the risk of → Uncertainty and show others: *I don't want this anymore. I want to stand with you. I want to listen to you. I want to take accountability. I want to meet you authentically. I will not judge you or put you down. I want you to be safe. I want to change with you. I don't know where this is going. Let's figure it out together.* They might ignore it, dismiss it or take it as an opportunity to put themselves above you. But they might also accept you, open up or join you. Sharing this book is that offer from me to you. Consider making the same offer to someone else, by striking up a conversation or by sharing this book with them. New spaces might open up that allow real connection with transformative potential – relationally, individually, and politically.

A Personal Note

It is a difficult balance how much space to take at all as someone with cis, white, male and class privilege to participate in feminist discourse. A lot of work went into keeping this short, and I do not think that my person should take much space here. But to honour the spirit of vulnerability and subjectivity, I do want to be open about why I wrote this and how my personal experience has affected my writing about these topics. For me, this process isn't a 'transformative journey', 'redemption', a fun adventure or some cool thing to do. It's work, and a lot of it is just weird and confusing and a bit exhausting. But it is really rewarding, and under no circumstance I would want to undo the changes that happened.

What among others Nora Samaran, bell hooks, Julia Serano and Mark Greene have to say about gender stirred up a deep sense that something has been kept from me since before I remember. Something that used to be a subconscious background noise became tangible and difficult to ignore. It has a history, a root. It stopped being how things just 'naturally' are.

I became acutely aware of my need to connect in a different way, but had no idea how to properly respond to that. I wanted to be done with the part of me that contributes to oppression as much as it does to my own isolation as fast as possible. My notes from that time, mostly based on intimate conversations with people sharing their experience, are really aggressive and accusative towards myself and anyone who embodies patriarchal masculinity. I tried to force it, not realising that patriarchal masculinity continues to fulfil an essential function in how I keep my life and relationships in balance. I could not see that my approach was ripe with the same mechanisms that I was trying to 'fight'. That backfired on me as much as on some of the people around me.

What does make a difference is the work from people close to me who turn towards me with honesty, understanding, kindness, patience and compassion. Not only to the parts of me that I neglected in the past, but especially those that I am trying to change. Equally helpful to me are my attempts to do the same for them. Going back through the notes that turned into this book and trying to at least partially replace judgement with a more compassionate attitude helped me tremendously.

There isn't a resolution – I am not 'transformed' into a secure 'new self'. The sense of certainty that exercising control grants doesn't carry over, and I don't think it should. This book is not intended to give an answer, it is meant to provide tools for not having one. Writing it is an attempt to pass some of the work and honest compassion that was granted to me on to the reader.

Sources

Adamczak, B. (2017). *Beziehungsweise Revolution: 1917, 1968 und kommende*. Suhrkamp Verlag.

Barker, M-J. (2020). *Sexuality: A Graphic Guide*. Icon Books.

Barker, M.-J., *The Consent Checklist*. Queer Square Zines.
www.rewriting-the-rules.com/zines

Barker, M.-J., *Staying with feelings*. Queer Square Zines.
www.rewriting-the-rules.com/zines

Bargetz, B., Scheele, A., & Schneider, S. (2019). *Umkämpfte Solidaritäten. Einleitung*. Femina Politica–Zeitschrift für feministische Politikwissenschaft, 28(2), 5-6.

Bee, M. (2004). *A Green Anarchist Project on Freedom and Love*. Green Anarchist #73–74.

Bierria, A. (Ed.) (2012). *Community accountability: Emerging movements to transform violence*. Social Justice, Vol. 37, No. 4 (122).

Butler, J., Gambetti, Z., & Sabsay, L. (Eds.). (2016). *Vulnerability in resistance*. Duke University Press.

Dean, J. (1995). *Reflective solidarity*. Constellations, 2(1), 114-140.

Doyle, J. E. S. (2019). *Care Work Is the Next Feminist Frontier*. GEN.
https://gen.medium.com/care-work-is-the-next-feminist-frontier-b50fbd8fde01

Ferguson, A., Hennessy, R., & Nagel, M. (2019). *Feminist Perspectives on Class and Work*. The Stanford Encyclopedia of Philosophy.

Fern, J. (2020). *Polysecure: Attachment, Trauma and Consensual Nonmonogamy*. Thorntree Press.

Graham, S. (2017). *Self consent: an introduction*. Love Uncommon Blog.
www.loveuncommon.com/2017/09/28/self-consent/

Greene, M. (2016). *Remaking Manhood: Stories from the Front Lines of Change*. CreateSpace Independent Publishing Platform.

Greene, M. (2018). The Little #MeToo Book for Men. Independently Published.

Hempstock, S., & Andry, S. (2017). *Radical Listening: A Manifesto*. Strike! Magazine

hooks, b. (2004). *The Will to Change: Men, Masculinity, and Love*. Atria Books.

Hutchinson, C. (2017). *Why Women Are Tired: The Price of Unpaid Emotional Labor.* The Huffington Post.

Johnson, S. (2011). *Hold Me Tight: Your Guide to the Most Successful Approach to Building Loving Relationships.* Little, Brown Book Group.

Lorde, A. (1988). *A Burst of Light.* Firebrand Books.

Meltsner, A. (2017). *Histories of Consent: Consent Culture and Community in Feminism and BDSM.* University of Vermont.

Samaran, N. (2019). *Turn This World Inside Out: The Emergence of Nurturance Culture.* AK Press.

Samaran, N. (2016a). *On Gaslighting.* Personal blog. https://norasamaran.com/2016/02/09/on-gaslighting/

Samaran, N. (2016b). *For Men who Desperately Need Autonomy.* Personal blog.
www.norasamaran.com/2016/07/21/for-men-who-desperately-need-autonomy-make-it-dont-take-it/

Serano, J. (2016). *Whipping Girl: A Transsexual Woman on Sexism and the Scapegoating of Femininity.* Basic Books.

Vandello, J. A., Bosson, J. K., Cohen, D., Burnaford, R. M., & Weaver, J. R. (2008). *Precarious manhood.* Journal of personality and social psychology, 95(6), 1325.

Smith, S. V., Plotkin, S. (2010). *Remaking Manhood: An Interview with Mark Greene*. Speaking of Sex with the Pleasure Mechanics Podcast.

Way, K. (2018). *I went on a date with Aziz Ansari. It turned into the worst night of my life*. Tab Media. www.babe.net/2018/01/13/aziz-ansari-28355

Witton, H. (2010). *Consent Culture and Intentional Relationships with Dr. Meg-John Barker*. Doing It with Hannah Witton Podcast.